31 MARKETING TIPS
Every Entrepreneur Needs To Know

Written by Tammy Fink

All rights reserved. Except for brief excerpts for review purposes, no part of this book may be reproduced or used in any form without written permission from the author.

The website addresses recommended throughout this book are offered as a resource to you. These websites are not intended in any way to be or imply an endorsement on the part of Tammy Fink or Blue Water Designs, LLC nor do we vouch for their content. I am not offering legal advice, I am only sharing my own experiences and knowledge.

ISBN: 9798682109814

©2020 Blue Water Designs, LLC

Author: Tammy Fink

Printed in the United States of America

First Edition 2020

I dedicate this book to you, because I created this book for YOU. Everything that has gone into creating it was done to inspire, encourage, and celebrate with you.

You've Got The Magic Within You,

I Believe In You...

Now Go & Create Something Extraordinary!

About the author

Trading in her career as a Corporate Designer in 2004, Tammy made a leap of faith when she started a full time freelance graphic design business. She started with a simple idea, and is now living her dream of owning an award-winning company, Blue Water Designs. She understands the struggles that many entrepreneurs undergo when starting their journey.

"I don't remember every dreaming of becoming an entrepreneur. I did dream of quitting my day job, but that's NOT the same thing." - Tammy Fink

Tammy Fink is an entrepreneur, professional speaker, author, and the chief WOW! creator, who specializes in client experience consulting. She is a 'loud, lovable, and full of laughs' online business personality who helps entrepreneurs create meaningful and memorable connections with their clients and customers. She has over 30 years of marketing, branding, and graphic design experience.

Tammy uses her unique perspective to help others navigate the sometimes confusing world of Small Business Marketing. When she wrote *31 Marketing Tips Every Entrepreneur Needs To Know*, she was writing it for someone just like you. She knows that you want to attract your ideal clients, the right way, at your own budget and investment level. She knows that most entrepreneurs start out doing everything by themselves, and that can get lonely. But it doesn't have to be, take the time to find your people. And learn from the best, they may not know everything, but chances are they are just a little higher up the mountain and can see a bit further than you can. Just keep pushing forward. You've got this, and always remember to keep Living The Dream .

TAMMY FINK – CHIEF WOW! CONSULTANT

CONTENTS

YOUR BRAND 2
UNIQUE POINT OF VIEW 3
FEATURES VS. BENEFITS: 6
BRAND CONSISTENCY 7
CROSS PROMOTIONS 10
DON'T DO IT ALL 11
AMAZING ADVERTISING 14
LOGO LOGO LOGO 15
IT'S ALL THE RAGE 18
OPEN FOR BUSINESS 19
DIAL+1-800 22
WHERE ARE YOU? 23
CLIENT HANGOUTS 26
TRUST IS EARNED 27
DOUBLE DAWG DARE YA 30
LEARN TO NETWORK 31
YOUR BRAND ISN'T YOUR LOGO 34
CELEBRATE YOUR CLIENTS 35
EMAIL MARKETING 38
EDUCATION GOES A LONG WAY 39
MARKETING MAGIC 42
GO, BE & DO LIVE 43
ELEVATOR PITCHES 46
KNOW YOUR AUDIENCE 47
ONLINE PRESENCE 50
MAINTAIN YOUR LOGO 51
EMAIL CAMPAIGNS 54
BUILD CONNECTIONS 55
SHOW & TELL 58
CREATE, RINSE & REPEAT 59
DON'T KEEP IT TO YOURSELF 62

YOUR BRAND

You should love what you do.

Owning your own business is different from working for someone else in many ways. For instance, when you are an employee you may not love your job. But, in order to have a successful brand you have to love what you do.

You cannot authentically promote what you don't love. Clients will see right through you.

And you must...

Absolutely, *without fail*

...USE YOUR OWN PRODUCT.

WHAT DO YOU DREAM OF CREATING?

_____
_____
_____
_____
_____
_____
_____
_____
_____
_____
_____
_____

> **❝** Don't limit yourself. Many people limit themselves to what they think they can do. You can go as far as your mind lets you. What you believe, remember, you can achieve."
>
> – Mary Kay Ash, Businesswoman

UNIQUE POINT OF VIEW

What makes your brand different?

Your brand can't be everything to everyone. Determine what makes your business different from your competitors. What specific problems do you solve for your clients? Once you've developed a unique selling point, it's your job to communicate it clearly and often.

WHAT IS YOUR UNIQUE POINT OF VIEW?

GOLD-NUGGET BONUS FORMULA:

HOW TO CONVERT A FEATURE TO A BENEFIT

Take a FEATURE + 'SO THAT' = Answer Becomes Your BENEFIT

For instance: Our cell phone services offer fast internet connection (feature), so that you can get information quickly when you need it (benefit).

FEATURES VS. BENEFITS

It's important to get this RIGHT from the start.

If you want to be successful in your market, then you must know the difference between features & benefits.

FEATURES are the facts about your products or services. **BENEFITS** are what your products or services *do* for your clients. And it's the benefits that you want to talk about, promote in ads, brochures, branding, and in everything that advertises to your client. Your clients want to know "what's in it for them". And it's your job to tell them.

LIST THE FEATURES:

LIST THE BENEFITS:

GOLD-NUGGET BONUS:

Is your message consistent?

Sometimes it can seem that you have been saying the same message over and over again. So perhaps you are considering changing it up, but this could decrease the power of your overall message. Once you have a strong point of view, you should be sure that your brand is known for that one thing...again and again. It becomes your 'number-one hit' song. And your fans want to hear it all of the time.

BRAND CONSISTENCY

Brand awareness is built on repetition.

All of your marketing materials should be consistent across every platform, whether it is your brochure, business card, or website.

Keep these consistent within all marketing:
- Contact Information
- High Resolution Logo
- Core Brand Message
- Professional Imagery
- Text Fonts
- Branding Colors

This doesn't mean that you can't try new things, just be sure that with each new campaign, to keep your brand identity consistent.

WHAT DO YOU NEED TO DO MORE OF WITH YOUR BRAND?

> "If you are starting your own business, the best shortcut is to find a good mentor."
>
> – Kim Kiyosaki, Entrepreneur

CROSS PROMOTIONS

Some things just go together.

Look for cross promotion opportunities. You can approach businesses that offer products and services that will complement your own. For instance, if you make gift baskets, you could ask a local florist to list your company link on their website, in exchange, you'll do the same for them. All businesses are ultimately looking to enhance their own client experience and brand touch points, so if you are able to contribute to this, it becomes a win-win for both companies.

Some products or services have obvious cross promotion opportunities. At other times, you may want to be creative. It will serve you well, if you are always on the lookout for opportunities to serve others.

WHO WOULD MAKE AN AMAZING PARTNERSHIP WITH YOU?

GOLD-NUGGET BONUS:

How do you tell them what you do?

If you can't explain it, how will they understand what it is that you do. You can start by describing something that they can relate to from who you help, and how you help them.

 For instance, when someone asks you what you do for a living, you might say, "Well, when someone starts a small business, they will need a sign in front of their building. I help them to create those signs. "

If you explain what it is that you do, clearly, perhaps the next time they hear of someone who needs a sign, they will think of you. Word of mouth advertising can be powerful, so use words that align with the results or product you offer.

DON'T DO IT ALL

Be strategic on social media.

It's easy to think targeting EVERY social media platform is the best option. This couldn't be further from the truth. The best way of targeting social media as a small business is to limit yourself to two or three social media sites. Consider, using Facebook, Twitter, Pinterest, Instagram, or LinkedIn to start. Then as you move forward, you can continue to expand and possibly even use their paid advertising to promote your business.

WHAT IS YOUR SOCIAL MEDIA ATTRACTION CHANNEL?

❝ Define success on your own terms, achieve it by your own rules, and build a life you're proud to live."

– Anne Sweeney, Disney Media Network - Co-Chair

AMAZING ADVERTISING

And the best part is that it's FREE?

Word of mouth advertising is FREE and is still the best way to get new clients. Keep your clients talking about your business to their friends by offering awesome customer service. Keeping your clients happy is a sure fire way to keep them coming back. People love to hear rave reviews from their peers, which encourages them to try your products and services for themselves.

Encourage online reviews when possible.

WHAT DO YOU DREAM OF CREATING?

> " A person who sees a problem is a human being; a person who finds a solution is visionary; and the person who goes out and does something about it is an entrepreneur."
>
> – Naveen Jain, InfoSpace Founder

LOGO LOGO LOGO

Now what did I do with it?

You've spent time and some of your hard earned money on a logo design. Now what do you do with it? You need to treat it as an investment. As soon as you get your logo, copy it to a CD or a memory stick. Then keep one copy in your office, and a second copy in a safety deposit box, or safe. Your logo is a precious part of your branding, and you should treat it like it is.

IS YOUR LOGO UP TO DATE? WHO NEEDS AN UPDATED VERSION OF YOUR LOGO? (PRINTER, ACCOUNTANT, SIGN COMPANY, WEBMASTER)?

> "The key to success is to start before you are ready."
>
> – Marie Forleo, American Entrepreneur

IT'S ALL THE RAGE

What are your clients saying?

People are more likely to buy from you if they see that others like them are patronizing your business. Get testimonials from happy clients and put it on your website or social media to drive more sales. You can request an email, or even better yet, ask them to do a quick video on their smart phone. The more authentic the better. You may ask them to use your product in the video.

WHO COULD WRITE YOU AN AMAZING TESTIMONIAL?

> "Starting a small business has been one of the best choices I ever made."
>
> – Rawa, Peachcake Founder

OPEN FOR BUSINESS

Are your clients opening your emails?

When you send an email to your client list, you could expect to get up to a 20 percent open rate. Here's a tip that could increase your open rate to 40 percent or more. After you send the first email, wait a week, and then change the subject line of the same email. You can now strategically re-send to the remaining unopened list. This has been proven to increase overall open rates across the board. Sometimes a simple idea can pay off big time.

WHAT EMAILS HAVE YOU SENT LATELY?

> "There is no better personal development tool than running your own business."
>
> – Ali Brown, Actor/Author

DIAL+1-800

Do you REALLY need an 800#?

800#'s are great for tracking marketing promotions, but aren't necessary for toll-free applications. Most people use cellphones, or have unlimited long distance on their land lines.

LIST ALL THE WAYS CLIENTS CAN CONTACT YOU INCLUDE CELL NUMBERS, EMAIL ADDRESSES, WEB ADDRESS, AND SOCIAL MEDIA LINKS)?

> *I wake up every morning and think to myself, 'How far can I push the company forward in the next 24 hours?"*
> – Leah Busque, TaskRabbit Founder

WHERE ARE YOU?

Free online marketing just around the corner.

Register your business with Google.com and BingPlaces.com to be sure your local business information is correct. This is the bare minimum that your clients expect to see online, so be sure it is accurate. Include your phone number, business hours, business description, address, map spot, and website link.

(You get bonus points for adding photos of your location and staff to personalize your profile even further).

WRITE A BRIEF DESCRIPTION OF YOUR BUSINESS THAT YOU CAN USE IN ALL OF YOUR MARKETING MATERIALS & ONLINE:

_____
_____
_____
_____
_____
_____
_____
_____
_____

GOLD-NUGGET BONUS:

What brands do your clients buy?

"By aligning yourself with trusted brands that your client's already purchase, you can attract more of the audience that you want," Tammy remarks. Are your clients coffee vs. wine drinkers, or American football vs. soccer fans? You can market to your client where they are already shopping.

The more you know about your clients the better you can align your offers and products with their buying habits.

CLIENT HANGOUTS

Do you know where they are?

Where do your clients get together - both online and offline? Look for communities and group activities where your target clients gather. By being involved in these communities, you will learn how to better communicate and market to your clients.

LIST PLACES WHERE YOUR CLIENTS COULD BE HANGING OUT:

> " Build your business success around something that you love — something that is inherently and endlessly interesting to you."
> – Martha Stewart, Martha Stewart Living Omnimedia

TRUST IS EARNED

People continue to do business with companies they trust.

A good way to build trust for your brand is to establish yourself as an expert in your field. You can enhance your clients experience by creating content on various online media platforms where your targeted clients are congregating.

Your target audience might enjoy:
- Blogs
- Videos
- Infographics
- Case Studies

The important thing is to make sure your content always offers value, so people will utilize it as a trusted resource. When people trust your content, they will trust your brand, product, and service.

EXAMPLE: If you are a travel agent, you might look for a wedding blog and offer to write a weekly "expert" column about honeymoon destinations, wedding venues, or other wedding resources.

WHAT ARE YOU AN EXPERT IN?

> "Courage doesn't always roar. Sometimes courage is the quiet voice at the end of the day saying, "I will try again tomorrow."
> – Mary Anne Radmacher, Author

DOUBLE DAWG DARE YA

Double opt-in clients are best.

You want to be sure that your client confirms their interest in receiving information from you via email. You don't want to get caught up in a permissions battle over spam accusations.

Any new subscriber should first be confirmed with a validation email, and only after the subscription has been confirmed should the email address be attached to your mailing list. Hence the term "double opt-in" – this way the user has to confirm, in two steps, their subscription or registration.

This step is important, not only because it truly confirms the user's intention, but it also ensures that the email address entered is valid.

NOTES:

> "True leadership stems from individuality that is honestly and sometimes imperfectly expressed... Leaders should strive for authenticity over perfection."
> – Sheryl Sandberg, Facebook COO

LEARN TO NETWORK

Like friends, clients are made.

You make friends by finding common interests, and spending time getting to know them. It's the same way with clients. Attend networking events in your area. Look and listen for opportunities where you can help. Don't automatically assume everyone needs your product or service. It's more about making relationships and solving problems.

LIST NETWORKING EVENTS IN YOUR AREA:

GOLD-NUGGET BONUS:

Logo Perspective?

"Entrepreneurs often dream about their logo first, " Tammy notes. "However the most overlooked thing about their logo is that it is much less about them, and more about how their logo should ATTRACT their ideal client."

So make your logo about your client, and make it clearly understood.

YOUR BRAND ISN'T YOUR LOGO

Your brand is a pinky promise.

While a logo is a brand's unique identity, it is not the whole picture. Your brand is your promise to deliver a positive experience to your client through quality service, product dependability, and much more. Your brand must deliver on these promises on every level of your business.

LOGO NOTES:

> "*Begin doing what you want to do now. We are not living in eternity. We have only this moment, sparkling like a star in our hand – and melting like a snowflake.*"
>
> – Marie Beyon Ray, Author

CELEBRATE YOUR CLIENTS

Developing milestones to encourage the people in your world.

When your clients celebrate you should be there to celebrate with them. It's important for them to know that you are a part of their world. Whether it is on social media, or in the real world let people know that they are amazing and deserve to be celebrated. Create and send a special card with a hand written note. Or you can even send a special email, or post a special graphic to their feed on social media. This way they know that you are on their team, and they will be thrilled to be on your team too.

LIST WAYS TO CELEBRATE YOUR CLIENTS:

GOLD-NUGGET BONUS:

Is your list current?

Every email should include a link so that the member is able to update their information. This will help to ensure that their information is both accurate and current.

EMAIL MARKETING

Building your list is very important.

Are you currently getting the email address of your existing clients? This is an awesome way to be sure that you stay on the minds of your clients. It is easier, and cheaper to keep your existing clients than to get new ones. Just ask for their email address for special offers or coupons that are only given to your email clients. You can also offer special "sign-up" opportunities that encourage your clients to give you their email addresses.

EMAIL NOTES:

GOLD-NUGGET BONUS EXAMPLE:

Teach what you know to your potential clients.

Men might be the ideal client for a auto repair shop. But, what could happen if they gave a "Hands On Car Care Workshop for WOMEN". They could even invite local women's organizations to participate in this general car maintenance education opportunity. Make it fun. Make it special. Maybe even wine and cheese. Most importantly, make it about creating a memorable experience for your clients.

EDUCATION GOES A LONG WAY

What do your clients want to know?

Is there a way that you can encourage your clients to learn more about your product? Workshops are a great way for your clients to interact with your brand.

You can meet the needs of a select group within your client base, while establishing yourself as an expert in your field and promoting your brand. It's a WIN-WIN situation for sure.

WORKSHOP IDEAS:

GOLD-NUGGET BONUS:

Use double-sided business cards.

Business cards are a good opportunity for a great first impression. Why not double your impact and use both sides of your business cards.

EXAMPLE: You can use a product photo for one side, and contact information, appointments, or reminders on the other.

MARKETING MAGIC

Do you have a card?

One of the least expensive ways to market yourself and your brand is to use business cards. I always ask for business cards. It's a sure way to get email addresses for your list. Be sure and ask if it is okay to email them before sending.

This is usually the time where they will ask you about your business, and then feel free to give them your card. It's easier to ask them about themselves first, this works great with business to business clients. I never leave a business conversation without asking for a business card.

LIST BUSINESS CARD INFORMATION:

_____
_____
_____
_____
_____
_____
_____
_____
_____
_____
_____

> "So often people are working hard at the wrong thing. Working on the right thing is probably more important than working hard."
>
> – Catrina Fake, Entrepreneur

GO, BE & DO LIVE

Are you going LIVE with your marketing?

Live video is quickly becoming one of the most popular features on many social media platforms, and it's not going away. Connect with your audience and future clients on live video in a way that only you can. It creates a unique client experience for everyone who sees it.

It doesn't have to be perfect. I remember the first time I pushed that GO LIVE button. It took me 15 minutes just to work up the nerve to do it those first few times myself. Just keep doing it…maybe just a sentence or two at the beginning. You will work through the problems of going LIVE and people want to support you while you are learning. Make your information valuable and it will give your brand an extra boost. You are giving your clients something they can relate to, and that makes you more likeable.

LIST IDEAS FOR LIVE TRAININGS, INSPIRATION, OR MOTIVATION VIDEOS:

ELEVATOR PITCHES

Aren't just for elevators anymore.

An elevator pitch/speech is a short description of your business that you could deliver in a short amount of time, like on an elevator ride. It should focus on results, and benefits for your clients. Even if you always take the stairs, you still need an elevator pitch.

WRONG:
"We sell copiers". (That's the product, not the benefit.)

BETTER: "We sell efficient copiers that will save you money". (Benefit, but not specific enough.)

BEST: We supply businesses with efficient copiers that will reduce their office costs by 50%.

WHAT IS YOUR ELEVATOR PITCH?

_____
_____
_____
_____
_____
_____
_____
_____

> " Surround yourself with a trusted and loyal team. It makes all the difference."
> – Alison Pincus, One Kings Lane Cofounder

KNOW YOUR AUDIENCE

What inspires them?

Marketing requires you to think outside the box and understand what your client actually wants. Most business owners are NOT their own typical client, and that's okay. **THINK** like your perfect client. Take time to get to know them. And discover what makes them buy from you.

WHAT DO YOU KNOW ABOUT YOUR CLIENTS?

GOLD-NUGGET BONUS:

Are you a maker...you may not need your own website?

There are third party websites that allow you to sell or market your products if they are handmade or created by you. Etsy.com, Zazzle.com, and Shopify.com offer a platform for a small fee that allows you to sell without having some of the headaches of running your own site. These sites take care of your payment gateway, some client service, and a low level of marketing.

ONLINE PRESENCE

Does your business really need a website?

There are 5 billion Google searches every day and over 1 billion active Facebook users. Some of those users are going to be interested in your business. You may or may not need an entire website, but you do need an online presence, such as a Facebook page, Google maps, Bing business page. You and your clients determine how much of an online presence you need.

LIST YOUR ONLINE PRESENT LOCATIONS:

GOLD-NUGGET BONUS:

How much should I spend on a logo?

When you are starting out, it's easy to just take the cheapest way out when it comes to your logo. But your logo is just as important as your location is if you have a brick and mortar store. It can be very expensive to rebrand later on. Decide on a budget, and get the best designer that you can afford. Plan on keeping the same logo for 3-5 years, before considering an update.

MAINTAIN YOUR LOGO

It's the face of your business.

Your logo is the face of your business on marketing materials. Ensure that it is presented cleanly and without distortion. Your logo's number one job is attracting your clients to your brand, so it needs to be attractive.

LOGO NOTES:

GOLD-NUGGET BONUS:

Branding through email.

To make a more powerful email impression, include your company logo (or company name) in your email signature. This will increase brand recognition.

You can also use your photo, social media links, website address, direct phone number, and anything else that makes is easy to connect with you. This helps to ensure your brand is consistent across all platforms.

EMAIL CAMPAIGNS

The next best thing to meeting for coffee.

Email. It's the one chance you have of speaking directly on an in-depth level with your target audience. It's also one of the cheapest ways. The only costs involved are the subscription fees charged by your online mailing platform. These costs are based on the size of your list. So, as a small business, you can pay less than $50 a month for the privilege of speaking to your raving fans.

LIST EMAIL CAMPAIGNS (WELCOME EMAILS, PROMOTIONS, PROGRAM LAUNCHES, OR HEY, JUST WANTED YOU TO KNOW THAT YOU ARE AMAZING EMAILS:

> "The difference between skill and talent: A skill is something you learn. Talent is what you can't help doing."
>
> – Caroline Ghosen, LEVO Founder

BUILD CONNECTIONS

Don't just share content, share lives.

Online Influencers' focus so much on creating self-promotional content they often forget to build connections. Building meaningful connections with your followers, fans, or clients helps you to utilize social media for it's intended purpose: socializing. It doesn't have to be all about business first. Learn to become invested in the lives of your people, and they will become your most loyal client base.

CONNECTION OPPORTUNITIES:

> "You are going to often find that to step into your biggest opportunity, you will be asked to move through your biggest fear or insecurity."
>
> – Ali Brown, Actor/Author

SHOW & TELL

Yep, you learned this in Kindergarten!

In building a brand, it is just as important that you **SHOW** your clients how to interact with your brand. You might do product sampling, video presentations, live demos, or other hands on activities.

TELL your clients about your products through multiple types of marketing materials. A website gives your clients immediate access to your products or services. While, a brochure gives you an effective leave behind for a prospective client.

WHAT CAN YOU SHOW & TELL?

> "Life-fulfilling work is never about the money — when you feel true passion for something, you instinctively find ways to nurture it."
>
> – Eileen Fisher, Fashion Designer

CREATE, RINSE & REPEAT

You don't have to always start from scratch.

Create core pieces of content that will help you to establish your point of view, your message, or even the solution to your client's problem. Once you have your core materials, use them in your marketing on social media, in postcards, website, even billboards. Spread your message in bite-sized nuggets. You can reuse and re-purpose everything from tips to checklists, videos to podcasts, blog posts to Insta-stories. Create the content, re-purpose it, and repeat the actions to develop your own marketing strategy.

HINT: And don't forget to document 'behind the scenes'. Your clients, fans, and members want to know how you make the magic happen.

CONTENT REPURPOSE PLANS:

GOLD-NUGGET BONUS:

Pay attention to your headlines.

Many people respond to the headline alone, no matter the content. So it really matters. A compelling headline will get you noticed, read, and shared. So take the time to research and build your headlines to attract your ideal client. Headlines can be used in emails, ads, banners, brochures., and social media posts. So make sure your headline gets you noticed.

DON'T KEEP IT TO YOURSELF

Some things are just meant to be shared.

Build your brand to be shared. Your clients, employees and even friends and family can help to share your brand. Once you have a clear picture of what your brand is, you can use marketing materials, articles, blog posts, photos, videos, and much more to increase your brand / product awareness.

SHARE YOUR BRAND IDEAS:

> "Connect to your clients by creating a pinky-promise with them through your marketing, branding, and overall client experience."
> – Tammy Fink, Chief WOW! Consultant

MY PINKY PROMISE

Marketing is a real struggle for a lot of entrepreneurs?

Marketing is the start of a conversation between you and your clients. While you want them to clearly know what it is that you do: {Obviously you are a ROCK STAR ENTREPRENEUR and have the best product and/or service on the planet}. But before you start your marketing, ask yourself: "What is it that my client wants"? "What is it that will change their world"? And "how can I offer a truly unique Customer Experience that will WOW! them?"

If you can learn to speak your client's language, and address their 'real world' problems, your marketing will feel like you are talking directly to them. And that my friend is the Magic of Marketing. Don't make it hard. Don't make it expensive.

Take the next month and implement as many of these tips as you can, it is my pinky promise to you that it will change how you look at Marketing forever. Focus on your clients first, and build relationships that will last a lifetime.

- Tammy Fink
Blue Water Designs & Supply Co.

Be sure and visit us at the BizBestiesCafe over on Facebook.
Where we are always caffeinated and highly engaging.

www.ingramcontent.com/pod-product-compliance
Lightning Source LLC
Chambersburg PA
CBHW051202220526
45473CB00003B/867